Where in the World Can I...

TRAIN TO GO
TO
THE MOON?

Where in the World Can I . . .
TRAIN TO GO
TO
THE MOON?
WORLD BOOK
www.worldbook.com

World Book, Inc.
180 North LaSalle Street, Suite 900
Chicago, Illinois 60601
USA

For information about other World Book publications, visit our website at **www.worldbook.com** or call **1-800-WORLDBK (967-5325).**

For information about sales to schools and libraries, call 1-800-975-3250 (United States), or 1-800-837-5365 (Canada).

Library of Congress Cataloging-in-Publication Data for this volume has been applied for.

Where in the World Can I…
ISBN: 978-0-7166-5251-9 (set, hc.)

Train to Go to the Moon?
ISBN: 978-0-7166-5256-4 (hc.)
ISBN: 978-0-7166-5268-7 (pf.)

Also available as:
ISBN: 978-0-7166-5262-5 (e-book)

STAFF

Executive Committee
President
  Geoff Broderick

Vice President, Editorial
  Tom Evans

Vice President, Finance
  Donald D. Keller

Vice President, International
  Eddy Kisman

Vice President, Technology
  Jason Dole

Director, Human Resources
  Bev Ecker

Editorial
Senior Editor
  Shawn Brennan

Curriculum Designer
  Caroline Davidson

Proofreader
  Nathalie Strassheim

Graphics and Design
Senior Visual Communications Designer
  Melanie Bender

Coordinator, Design Development and Production
  Brenda Tropinski

Senior Media Editor
  Rosalia Bledsoe

Acknowledgments
Writer: Cynthia O'Brien

Produced by
Focus Strategic
Communications Inc.

TABLE OF CONTENTS

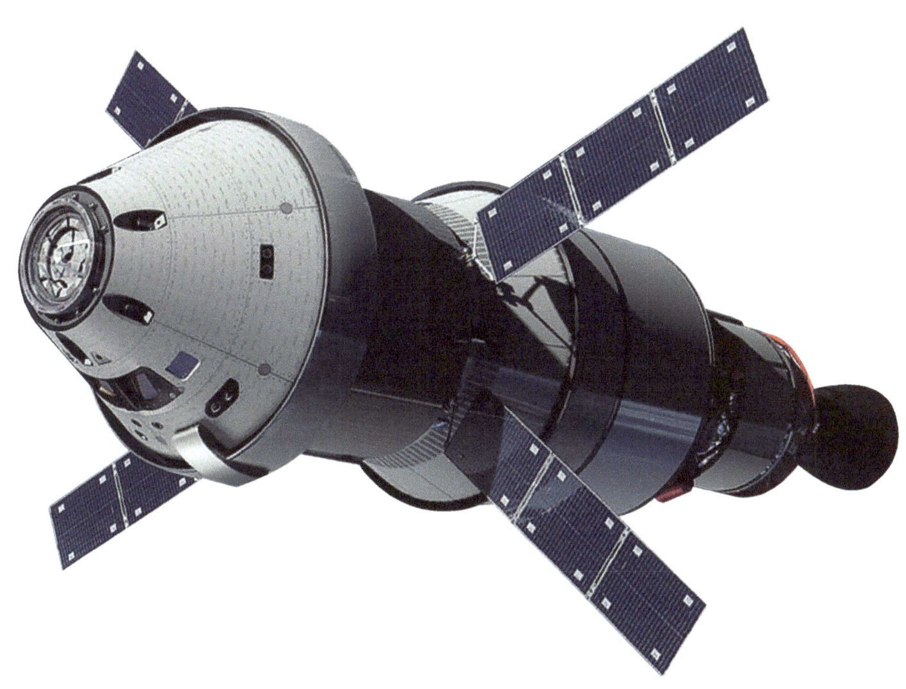

TO THE
MOON!

If you look up in the night sky, the moon is the largest, brightest object you can see. This rocky sphere is Earth's closest neighbor in space. The moon lies about 239,000 miles (385,000 kilometers) away from our planet. It is Earth's only natural *satellite*. A satellite is something that *orbits* (travels around) something else. The moon does a full, oval-shaped orbit around Earth every 27.3 days. At the same time, Earth orbits the sun.

The moon probably formed
about 4.6 billion years ago,
soon after Earth. Scientists think
that an object about the size of
the planet Mars collided with
Earth. This crash caused
vaporized rock (rock that is so
hot it turns to a gas) and other
debris to fly out into space.
As the rock and debris orbited
Earth, it cooled and came
together to form the moon.
The moon is about one quarter
the size of Earth.

The moon looks bright, but it does not make its own light.
It reflects light from the sun. The sun lights up different parts of
the moon as it orbits Earth. We can hardly see the first stage—
the new moon—because the sun is lighting up the side of the
moon we cannot see from Earth. Then the moon appears to get
bigger until it becomes a full moon. Over the next phases, the
moon seems to get smaller until there is another new moon.

The moon is covered in millions of small and large *craters* (round indents in the moon's surface). Such rocky objects as asteroids and *comets* (combinations of frozen gases, rock, and dust) crashed into the moon and created them.

Dark areas on the surface, called *maria*, are huge craters. The craters are filled with hardened *lava* (hot, liquid rock from volcanoes) from volcano eruptions that happened billions of years ago.

Ancient people stared up at the moon
in awe. Some people thought the moon
was a god or goddess that controlled
things on Earth.
Others noticed
the moon's phases
and used them to
mark time and create
calendars.

Ancient Greek
astronomers (scientists
who study the universe
and objects in it) were
the first to know that
the moon reflected
light from the sun.

But they also got some things wrong. For
hundreds of years, people believed that the
moon and the sun orbited Earth. They also
believed the moon had a smooth surface.

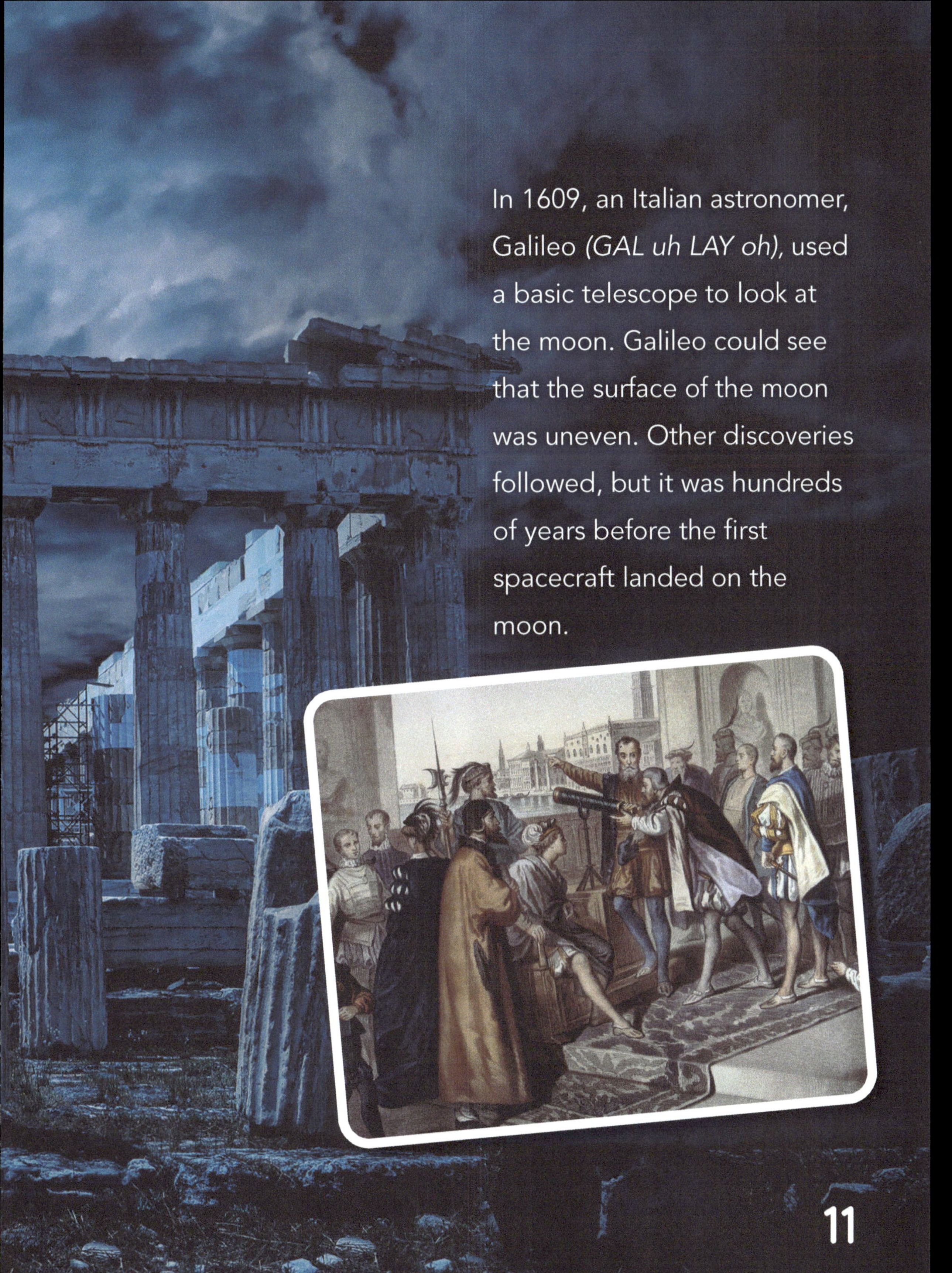

In 1609, an Italian astronomer, Galileo *(GAL uh LAY oh)*, used a basic telescope to look at the moon. Galileo could see that the surface of the moon was uneven. Other discoveries followed, but it was hundreds of years before the first spacecraft landed on the moon.

In January 1959, the Soviet Union launched
the first Luna *probe*. A probe is an unmanned
spacecraft that collects scientific information to
send back to Earth. Luna 1 passed near the
moon, and Luna 2 was the first probe to strike
the moon's surface. Other Luna missions
followed.

Meanwhile, the United States had established
NASA (National Aeronautics and Space
Administration) in 1958. NASA launched nine
Ranger missions in the early 1960's and seven
Surveyor missions in the later 1960's. These
and other missions helped
pave the way for
the Apollo missions.

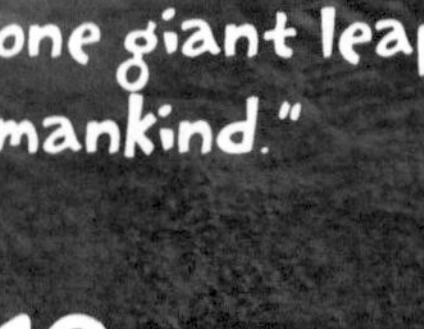

Yuri Gagarin, from the Soviet Union, became the first human in space in April 1961. Gagarin's spacecraft orbited Earth.

NASA's Apollo 8 mission sent three astronauts on an orbit around the moon in December 1968. Less than a year later, the Apollo 11 mission was the first to land people on the moon. The Eagle, a lunar module, landed on a flat area of the moon called the Sea of Tranquility.

On July 20, 1969, Neil Armstrong and Edwin (Buzz) Aldrin became the first men to set foot on the moon.

After the successful Apollo 11 landing, five more Apollo missions landed men on the moon. On each mission, one astronaut stayed in the command module. Two other astronauts landed the lunar module on the moon's surface. A total of twelve men have landed on the moon so far. They took many photographs and brought back samples of moon rock.

Apollo 11

July 16-July 24, 1969

Command module pilot: Michael Collins

Commander: Neil Alden Armstrong

Lunar module pilot: Edwin (Buzz) Aldrin

Apollo 12

November 14-November 24, 1969

Command module pilot: Richard F. Gordon, Jr.

Commander: Charles Conrad, Jr.

Lunar module pilot: Alan L. Bean

Apollo 14

January 31-February 9, 1971

Command module pilot: Stuart Allen Roosa

Commander: Alan B. Shepard, Jr.

Lunar module pilot: Edgar D. Mitchell

Apollo 15

July 26-August 7, 1971

Command module pilot: Alfred Merrill Worden

Commander: David R. Scott

Lunar module pilot: James B. Irwin

Apollo 16

April 16-April 27, 1972

Command module pilot: Thomas K. Mattingly II

Commander: John W. Young

Lunar module pilot: Charles Moss Duke, Jr.

Apollo 17

December 7-December 19, 1972

Command module pilot: Ronald E. Evans, Jr.

Commander: Eugene Andrew Cernan

Lunar module pilot: Harrison H. Schmitt

After Apollo 17, there were no moon missions for many years. But since the 1990's, special spacecraft have been exploring and sending information back to Earth. We now know a lot more. For example, we know that there is water on the moon. Future astronauts may be able to use it when they visit.

In 2019, China's Chang'e 4 mission became the first to land a spacecraft on the far side of the moon. Its Yutu-2 *rover* traveled around on the moon's surface. Rovers are unmanned robotic vehicles.

They take photographs, analyze information, and dig up
samples. NASA's Artemis program focuses on sending
people to the moon again and preparing to land humans
on Mars.

One day, you may be able to board a train or a rocket to
the moon. In the meantime, keep reading to see where
you can go on a space adventure right now!

CHINESE LUNAR EXPLORATION PROGRAM

In October 2007, China
launched the first of the
Chang'e moon missions.
Chang'e 1 and 2 orbited the
moon. Later missions landed or
will land on the moon. China
also plans to send astronauts
to the moon in the future.

CAMP KENNEDY
SPACE CENTER

You will feel like a real astronaut in training at Camp Kennedy Space Center (Camp KSC®). The weeklong day camp is held at NASA's Kennedy Space Center, about 50 miles (80 kilometers) east of Orlando, on Merritt Island, Florida. This area is part of Florida's Space Coast. All spacecraft that carry crew launch from the Kennedy Space Center, including the Apollo rockets to the moon. The U.S. Space Force is based at nearby Cape Canaveral Space Force Station.

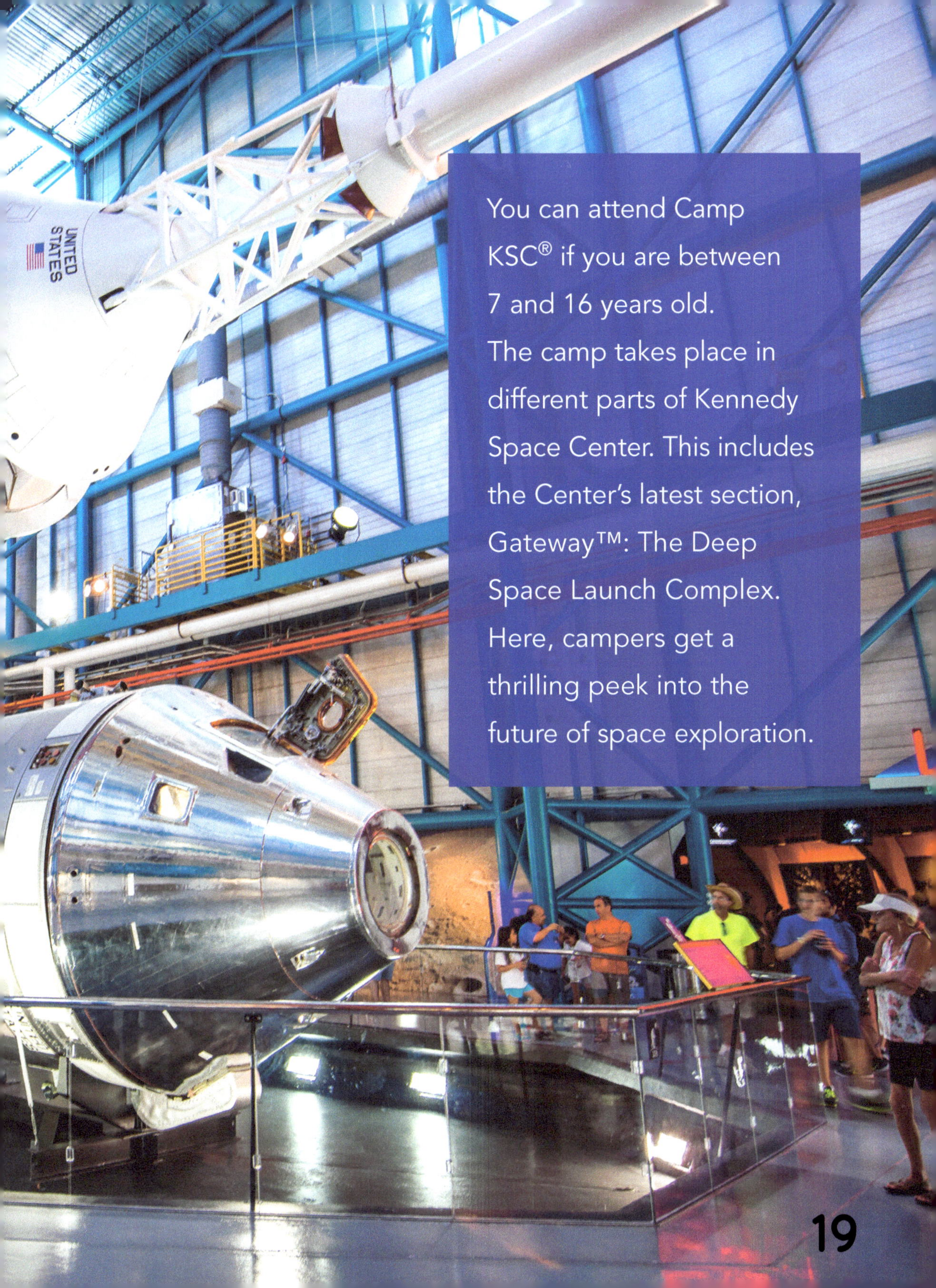

You can attend Camp KSC® if you are between 7 and 16 years old. The camp takes place in different parts of Kennedy Space Center. This includes the Center's latest section, Gateway™: The Deep Space Launch Complex. Here, campers get a thrilling peek into the future of space exploration.

Astronauts must go through years of training. But you can skip to the front of the class at the Astronaut Training Experience (ATX)®. Here, you and the other campers are in charge of launching and docking NASA's Space Launch System (SLS) rocket. It all happens in a *simulated environment* (conditions created to imitate something real). So even though you are not launching a real rocket, it will feel like you are!

Just like real astronaut training, ATX®
is all about teamwork. Some campers
will be launch controllers, while others
are part of the Orion capsule crew.
Many real-life missions encounter
problems or emergency situations.

The ATX® mission is no different.
Launch controllers and capsule crew
members will be given one or two
problems to solve during their
adventure. By working with each
other, the team finds the solutions to
launch and dock the rocket safely.

When a rocket soars into space, it is breaking away from the pull of Earth's *gravity*. Gravity is an invisible force that pulls things toward each other. It makes things fall.

It keeps your feet on the ground instead of floating away. In space, astronauts learn to deal with a condition called microgravity (*micro* means very small). They feel like they are weightless and floating.

As part of your astronaut training, you learn what it is like to feel weightless. ATX® has a specially made microgravity chair, also called the "spacewalk" chair. The chair hovers over the floor, giving you the feeling of free falling in space. Just as astronauts are tied to the spacecraft, straps keep you and the chair tied together while you complete repairs to a reconstructed part of the Space Station.

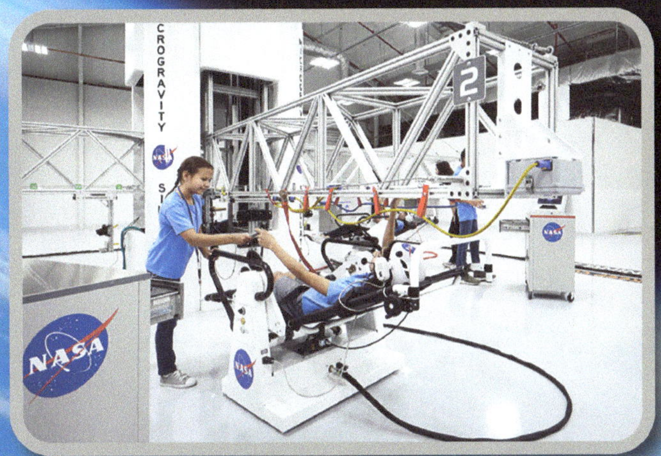

Could you handle a mission to Mars? Find out by using the camp's virtual reality equipment. The special eyewear transports you to the Red Planet to explore and walk on its surface. You will communicate with mission control to report your findings.

Scientists and space engineers are already working on plans to land humans on Mars. Many unmanned spacecraft have traveled to Mars already. Rovers have been exploring the planet's surface since 1997. The largest and newest rover—Perseverance—landed on Mars on February 18, 2021. The robot is collecting rock and soil samples that may be returned to Earth later. It also has a tool that will try to make oxygen. People need oxygen to breathe, so this tool may be very useful when astronauts visit Mars.

Once you have learned how to walk on Mars, take a trip to Mars Base 1. Mars is very cold and can be very windy. At the Base Operations Center, you will learn how astronauts might survive on this planet. You will deal with a spacecraft crash landing and send rovers out to explore. In the Botany Lab, you will learn about NASA's experiments with growing vegetables indoors. In the Engineering Lab, you and your team will program robots to clean up after a dust storm.

In between trips into space, your time at Camp KSC® will be full of other activities. You can see the Saturn V Moon Rocket and the Space Shuttle Atlantis up close. There is a tour to the Astronauts Hall of Fame®, and you might even meet an astronaut in person. At the end of the week, you will have earned an official Camp KSC® certificate.

SPACE CAMP

The U.S. Space & Rocket Center®, in Huntsville, Alabama, hosts Space Camp. This amazing experience allows campers to stay for six days and five nights. The Center houses one of the world's largest collections of rockets. Huntsville is called "Rocket City" because scientists designed and tested the Saturn V rocket here. Saturn V was the rocket that carried people to the moon for the first time.

Since Space Camp started in 1982, people from all over the world have come to train there. It has inspired many people to become NASA and ESA (European Space Agency) astronauts, scientists, and engineers.

Astronaut training helps to prepare space explorers
for many situations. They need to deal with changes
in gravity conditions, adjust to flying inside a
spacecraft, and do repairs while outside the craft.

When you arrive at Space Camp, you will receive some of the same training as NASA astronauts. NASA helped to design the training equipment at the camp. This means it is as close as possible to the real thing.

At Space Camp, you can try out the gravity chair to see how it feels to be weightless while you walk on the moon. Then take a spin in the multi-axis trainer. It will feel like you are inside a spacecraft hurtling through space!

To experience a spacewalk outside of the spacecraft, take a seat in the *MMU* (Manned Maneuvering Unit) simulator. An MMU operates as a backpack *propulsion* (force that moves something forward) device. Astronauts use these to hover in space without being tied to the spacecraft.

The International Space Station
(ISS) is a large spacecraft that
orbits Earth. Six astronauts
at once can live there for periods
of time. They do research and
science experiments on board.
It is an international station because
many countries worked together
to build it. The first residential
crew arrived aboard on November 2,
2000, and people have lived there
ever since.

Older trainees at Space Camp
will find out what it is like to live
on board the ISS. Part of this
experience involves keeping
the ISS in good condition.
Space Camp has set up a simulated
repair mission just for campers.

The mission involves suiting up in a spacesuit and spacewalking around the *replica* (copy) of a small part of the Space Station. An important part of the mission is teamwork. A successful mission means solving problems both with crew in the control room and with the others working on repairs.

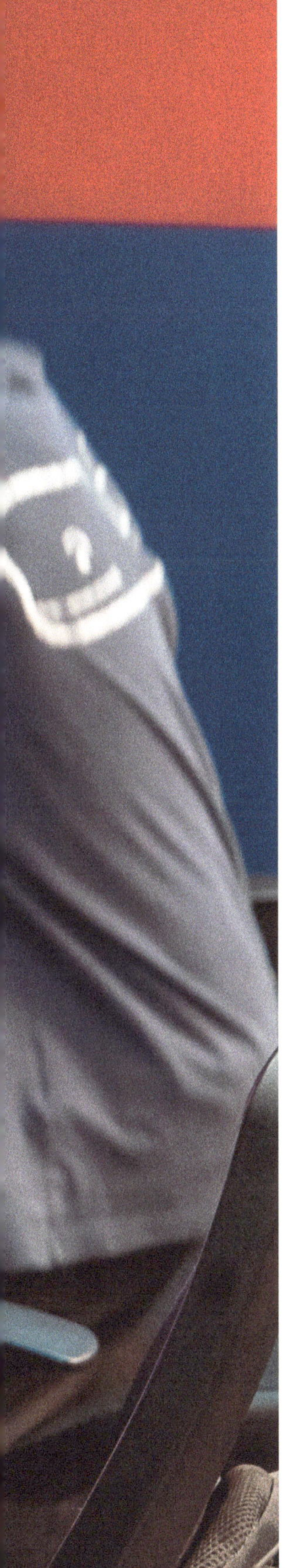

Do you dream of building rockets? The instructors at Space Camp will teach you how to build—and launch!—your own rocket. The rockets are made from paper rolled around a tube and topped with a cone that helps with speed.

Once you select and make a fin shape, you will attach these to the rocket. The fins help with direction and to keep your rocket stable. No space rocket launches without tests, so you will test your rocket before the big launch. You may have to make some changes, but then get ready to see it soar!

NASA's Artemis program is working on sending people to the moon. Plans also include building a moon base camp and a space station called Gateway, and landing astronauts on Mars. Astronauts will travel on board the Orion spacecraft. It will launch from the world's most powerful rocket system (NASA's Space Launch System rocket).

Space Camp has a life-size model of an Orion spacecraft. Campers will work as a team to launch Orion on a mission to Mars. They will work both as astronauts in the spacecraft, as well as controllers. Campers will also learn how to build a place to live on Mars.

If you continue your training
after Space Camp, maybe
you will be one of the
astronauts to visit Mars!

SPACE FLIGHT ACADEMY

If you're between 11 and 16 years old, check out Virginia Space Flight Academy in Wallops Island, Virginia. This is a residential camp, which means you stay for five nights and six days. Depending on your interests, you can choose to attend the Space Adventure Camp or the Advanced Rocketry Camp. Both camps include rocket building and launching activities.

The camps are held near the NASA Wallops Flight Facility. The Wallops Flight Facility is a NASA launch site for all kinds of missions. Cygnus, a resupply spacecraft, has been launched from here to the International Space Station. Campers will have a chance to visit the facility during their week. They stay in cabins at the Chincoteague Bay Field Station.

Robots are important tools in space exploration. The Mars rovers, like Perseverance, are robots. They can move around, pick up samples, take photos, analyze information, and much more. Small robots, like NASA's A-PUFFER, can flatten themselves to get into tight spaces.

Humanoid robots (robots that look like people) may help to build a base on the moon or Mars. Unlike humans, robots do not need to breathe, eat, or sleep. They can withstand extreme temperatures and do things that are too dangerous for astronauts to attempt.

At the Space Adventure Camp, you will learn about coding and robotics using LEGO Mindstorms® EV3 kits. This is the chance to design, build, and program your very own robot. You will also learn about *drones* (unmanned flying robots) and take part in a drone challenge.

It's a thrill to watch a rocket launch, especially when you have built the rocket yourself. Rocket building—and launching—is a big part of Space Adventure Camp. You can make more than one rocket, using a model kit or building your own. To design your own, you will learn how to use *CAD* (computer-aided design) and how to print your parts on a 3-D printer.

Field trips are a fun part of
the Space Flight Academy
camp experience. Campers
will see a real rocket launch
pad and a hangar where
rockets are built.

They will also visit the
National Oceanic and
Atmospheric Administration
(NOAA) weather facility, the
Rocket Lab, and the U.S.
Navy's Surface Combat
System Center.

The Wallops Flight Facility
and NOAA cooperate with
certain launches, such
as scientific balloons.

There are also engineering competitions and an astronomy night, where campers will see telescope images and learn about constellations, the planets, and more.

At the end of the week, there is a graduation and awards ceremony where you will receive your very own certificate from the Space Flight Academy.

READING FOCUS

Text Structure is all about the way a text is organized. When we know the structure, we can focus more of our energy and attention on comprehending what we read.

This book uses a Description Text Structure. It describes a topic and its characteristics using details, adjectives, and a logical order. Description texts often use examples to show and explain the main idea or topic.

Description texts usually include a lot of interesting details. We can use a graphic organizer to help us keep track of the most important information.

1. This is a Bubble Diagram, a strong graphic organizer for Description texts. Visit **www.worldbook.com/resources** to download and print copies or create your own!

2. As you read and/or revisit the text, complete a Bubble Diagram for EACH section:
   - To the Moon!
   - Chinese Lunar Exploration Program
   - Camp Kennedy Space Center
   - Space Camp
   - Virginia Space Flight Academy

3. For each section, write the title in the center-most bubble. Next, add important details to the bubbles attached to that central, main idea. Remember, you do not have enough bubbles for *every* detail. Think critically to determine which details to include.

What other information about training to go to the moon will you add to your Bubble Diagram?

WRITING FOCUS

What do YOU think?

In your opinion, which of the four spotlighted locations would be best for training to go to the moon?

Review the notes you took on your Bubble Diagrams. Use evidence from the text, supported by logical reasoning, to answer the question. Your writing should include:

- A **hook** where you grab your readers' attention

- A **thesis statement** where you state your opinion

- At least 3 **reasons** why that is your opinion

- At least 3 **details** that support each reason

Use an Opinion Writing Graphic Organizer to sort through your thoughts before you write your response. Create your own or download and print a version from **www.worldbook.com/ resources.**

Opinion Writing Graphic Organizer

Hook and Thesis:	Reason #1	Detail #1
		Detail #2
		Detail #3
	Reason #2	Detail #1
		Detail #2
		Detail #3
	Reason #3	Detail #1
		Detail #2
		Detail #3

You might have noticed some words in this book written in *italics*. That means they are vocabulary terms! **Challenge yourself!** Can you include at least 5 of these words in your opinion writing?

INDEX

ACKNOWLEDGMENTS

Cover: © Sergey Nivens, Shutterstock
TP: © Elena11, Shutterstock
6–7 © Paitoon Pornsuksomboon, Shutterstock
8–9 © HelenField, Shutterstock; © Elena11, Shutterstock
10–11 © Viacheslav Lopatin, Shutterstock; © Index/Heritage Images, Alamy
12–13 © Photo Researchers, Alamy; NASA
14–15 © HelenField, Shutterstock; NASA
16–17 © Kevin Gill, Flickr
18–19 © NaughtyNut, Shutterstock
20–21 © Dima Zel, Shutterstock; © Tran Thu Hang, Shutterstock
22–23 © Artsiom Petrushenka, Shutterstock; Kennedy Space Center
24–25 © Anterovium, Shutterstock; © Jurik Peter, Shutterstock
26–27 © EWY Media, Shutterstock
28–29 © KK.KICKIN, Shutterstock; © Tim Daugherty, Shutterstock
30–31 © Vladi333, Shutterstock; © Space Camp/U.S. Space & Rocket Center
32–33 © Vadim Sadovski, Shutterstock; © Space Camp/U.S. Space & Rocket Center
34–35 © Space Camp/U.S. Space & Rocket Center; © Amanda Shavers, Associated Press
36–37 © Dima Zel, Shutterstock
38–39 © J Marshall/Tribaleye Images, Alamy
40–41 © Peter Ekvall, Alamy
42–43 © Michael Doolittle, Alamy; © Marlon Lopez MMG1 Design, Shutterstock
44–45 © PhoCas Travel, Shutterstock

www.ingramcontent.com/pod-product-compliance
Lightning Source LLC
Chambersburg PA
CBHW042206030726
47599CB00023B/710